BIRDS OF A FEATHER

by Angela "Niecy"

Illustrated by Erica Ramsey-Bowen

ISBN 978-1-63814-547-9 (Paperback)
ISBN 978-1-63814-548-6 (Digital)

Covenant Books
11661 Hwy 707
Murrells Inlet, SC 29576
www.covenantbooks.com

THIS BOOK BELONGS TO:

_____

I dedicate this book
to children of all ages
Inspired by my
hatchling's hatchlings
Once you learn to fly
Trust your ability to soar
The wind will do the rest
Enjoy the journey

This story being told
happens to be true.

Find the lesson in the
three amigos' coo.

$\mathcal{I}$t happened one summer,
My daughter Jameela's
major bummer.

Out of nowhere, needing a place to nest,

Is my youngest of three with her children and pets

A parakeet trio

Draped in feathers,

Looking straight out of Rio.

The dominant bird is
Tweety, the only male.
Yellow is his color
from head to tail.

Stormy looks like the sky,
on a cloudy day.

Lucky's name suited her nature
all the way.

They didn't always get along,
in the space they lived daily.
Even though their behavior,
Was somewhat scaly.

Placed on the balcony for fresh
air from time to time,
To the top of the cage, two of the
three would often climb.

Possibly to discover an open door,
Or begin an adventure, the world to explore.

One day on the balcony, while
planting flowers and sage,
I must have created an opening
when adjusting the cage.

I did not notice the gap, which was ever so slight,
As I gazed at the planted garden with sheer delight.

As the day was ending with the setting of the sun,
Jameela noticed, instead of three
birds, there was only one.

I had no idea the cage had opened
and two had taken flight.
Stormy and Tweety had flown away into the night.

Surprised and alarmed, we wondered what happened
Yet kept our cool to avoid snappin'.

Were they hurt or eaten by a bird of prey,
Possibly by the falcon that came
lurking just the other day?

We didn't want to alarm or give the kids a fright
Though deep inside I knew Stormy
and Tweety were all right.

If Lucky could, what would she say?
Where did they go? Why did she stay?
Did she warn them not to go,
Or did they ask her, too, and she said no?

With Lucky inside as we settled to sleep,
After a prayer together, we didn't hear a peep.

We woke to check the balcony
if the birds were back
After escaping last night
because a little cage crack.

We'd already decided to take
an easy Sunday morning
After our birds took flight
without a warning.

13

Lucky woke chirping lively and strong.
Could there be something outside going on?

The notion came to place her back outside,
Secured her cage and allowed her to guide.

That's exactly what happened as Lucky sang.
Though Tweety was spotted first,
Stormy returned first of the gang.

Eventually, Tweety decided to reunite.
To our amazement, the duo made it through the night.

Three birds of a feather back together
Through thick and thin, no matter the weather.

Their journey landed them home safely to stay,
Demonstrating prayer works—namaste.

The End

CPSIA information can be obtained
at www.ICGtesting.com
Printed in the USA
JSHW041642290123
36808JS00002B/12